Other Snapshot Series Books

People, Trees and Poverty:
A Snapshot of Environmental Missions
Lowell Bliss

People, Trees & Poverty shares a high-level overview of what it looks like to reach the unreached through advocacy on environmental issues. However, this book does more than raise awareness and pluck your heartstrings. It concludes with a critical feature, listing additional resources, gatherings, and organizations to move the reader from concern to action.

It's Your Call:
To a Missional or Missionary Life
David P. Jacob

For most believers, several factors influence their missions call. Some are called to stay in their hometown and support missions at their local church, others are called to short-term mission trips, while others are called to spend a lifetime overseas. *It's Your Call* highlights three things that can help you discover the adventure God has for you in his mission: prayer and Bible study, missionary mentorship, and short-term mission trips.

Insiders and Alongsiders:
An Invitation to the Conversation
Kevin Higgins

In *Insiders and Alongsiders*, Kevin Higgins offers his evolving perspective on "insider" movements (IMs), a controversial type of movement in which families and friendship networks become faithful followers of Jesus while remaining identified with the culture of their people group.

Effective Spiritual Warfare: Wrestling in God's Strength

Mary Lou Codman-Wilson

Effective Spiritual Warfare describes the tactics evil forces use to keep Christians from fulfilling God's plans for them personally and globally. Then the book concentrates primarily on eight ways to overcome Satan in our lives. These principles are truly life transforming, thoroughly biblical, and consistently validated throughout Christian history.

Freedom From Exploitation: Christian Responses to Moden-Day Slavery

Marion S. Carson

Authoritative and deeply compassionate, *Freedom from Exploitation* offers an actionable roadmap for believers in pursuit of justice and mercy. Drawing from biblical principles and contemporary examples, it urges the church to transcend complacency and embody Christ's teachings. The insights within these pages will guide Christian communities in taking up the cause for the oppressed, equipping them to make a tangible difference.

Endorsements

Lewie Clark issues a wakeup call to today's church that if we really want to follow the model of Jesus and the early church, we should be empowering singles for kingdom ministry without presuming they first need to be married. This book is a thoughtful journey that will both encourage single adults that they are fully qualified and equipped for kingdom leadership while simultaneously reminding us all what the true family of believers is all about.

Rev. **Barry N. Danylak**, PhD
Executive Director, SEE Globally

The lies we believe influence our thinking and behavior without our conscious awareness. But when these lies get exposed and rejected, we have opportunity to joyfully embrace fresh, wholesome thinking and relating. Lewie's book powerfully exposes cultural lies that cripple the lives and ministries of many singles. It empowers members of Christ's family to value the unique freedoms that singles enjoy, at times, giving them an advantage over married Christian workers. I am excited to give this book to friends who are single and to those in Christian leadership so that our cultural lies can be exposed and rejected. Let's trash the shame and marginalization of singles. Let's embrace them as fully complete in Christ. Let's leverage their advantages for the extension of God's kingdom. You will know the truth and the truth will set you free (John 8:38).

Albert Ehmann
Church planter, leader, and mentor for 55 years

Would your church hire single Saint Paul as pastor? How about young unwed Amy Carmichael to lead a mission? The data says no, and that's not just bad for all our Amys and Pauls—it's a disaster for the spread of the gospel. Sociological headwinds are converging. We must stop sidelining our fastest growing demographic. This book is a wakeup call to Protestants to rethink the sacred role of celibacy for mission.

Del Fehsenfeld III
Life Action Ministries

As the World Evangelical Alliance begins to advance a paradigm that fully values, engages, and empowers single and single-again evangelicals, I have turned to Lewie many times for encouragement and advice. I have read *Single-Minded Service* as a book, but also as a life—Lewie's life. May you likewise be encouraged, and more so, challenged by Lewie's writing, and should the Lord give you favor to know him, and his life.

Mark McLeod
Singles Advocacy Initiative, WEA

Today, most Christians assume that marriage is a fundamental prerequisite for leadership in the church. But Lewie Clark sheds light on how singles have frequently been the spearheads of Christ's kingdom, ever since the church's beginning. This wonderful book will empower singles to love, serve, and lead the body of Christ.

Seth Osborn, PhD
Adjunct Professor, Indiana Wesleyan University

The bias is real. I spent years helping hundreds of churches find senior pastors, and not one of them would consider an unmarried candidate. And yet for more than forty years, I've watched Lewie Clark pastor, lead, and disciple others (myself included). As a single, never-married man, the biblical insights Lewie brings regarding singleness need to be heard by the church.

Tim Stevens
CEO & Founder, LeadingSmart

SINGLE-MINDED SERVICE

Recovering the Essential Role
of Singles
in Kingdom Leadership

Lewie Clark
with Tim Grissom

visit us at missionbooks.org

Single-Minded Service:
Rediscovering the Essential Role of Singles in Kingdom Leadership

© 2024 by Lewie Clark. All Rights Reserved.

No part of this book may be reproduced, stored in a retrieval system, or transmitted in any form or by any means—electronic, mechanical, photocopy, recording, or otherwise—without prior written permission from the publisher, except brief quotations used in connection with reviews. This manuscript may not be entered into AI, even for AI training. For permission, email permissions@wclbooks.com. For corrections, email editor@wclbooks.com.

William Carey Publishing (WCP) publishes resources to shape and advance the missiological conversation in the world. We publish a broad range of thought-provoking books and do not necessarily endorse all opinions set forth here or in works referenced within this book.

The URLs included in this book are provided for personal use only and are current as of the date of publication, but the publisher disclaims any obligation to update them after publication.

Scriptures are taken from the Holy Bible, New International Version®, NIV®. Copyright © 1973, 1978, 1984, 2011 by Biblica, Inc.™ Used by permission of Zondervan. All rights reserved worldwide. www.zondervan.com. The "NIV" and "New International Version" are trademarks registered in the United States Patent and Trademark Office by Biblica, Inc.™

Published by William Carey Publishing
10 W. Dry Creek Cir
Littleton, CO 80120 | www.missionbooks.org

William Carey Publishing is a ministry of Frontier Ventures
Pasadena, CA | www.frontierventures.org

Cover and Interior Designer: Mike Riester

ISBNs: 978-1-64508-655-0 (paperback), 978-1-64508-614-7 (epub)

Printed Worldwide   28 27 26 25 24   1 2 3 4 5   IN

Library of Congress Control Number: 2024950168

Contents

Finding Our Way   1

The Bias   9

The Invisible Single   19

A Theology of Singleness   31

The Kingdom-First Life   43

Being Barnabas   51

1
Finding Our Way

I live in Chicago, a place where 2.7 million people share 234 square miles, 4,000 miles of public roadway, and a 1,900-mile alley system. We have two international airports: Chicago O'Hare and Chicago Midway. O'Hare is ranked the second busiest airport in the nation and the sixth busiest in the world. And speaking of going places, between its buses and trains, the Chicago Transit Authority provides 1.7 million rides on an average weekday.

Chicago is a big place with a lot of people and all kinds of ways to get around: car, taxi, ride-share, bus, train, bike (we have over 300 miles of bike lanes, by the way), walking, and even water taxi.

I'll just come right out and say it: I love my city.

But even after spending most of my life in Chicagoland (as we like to call it), I still need directions when I'm in an unfamiliar part of the city. I often rely on GPS to tell me the best route to take and what the public transportation options are. As much as I love Chicago, I hate not knowing where I am even more.

SINGLE-MINDED SERVICE

When I was in Calgary a few years ago, I was thinking about my dependence on GPS and the constant need to know where I am. I was there speaking at a conference about singles and their role in building God's kingdom. As I began to speak, it occurred to me that there was a connection between my unfamiliarity with Calgary and the disorientation of singles in the church: we're in bad need of direction. I could no more navigate my way around an unfamiliar city to me, without GPS or a guide, than the average Christian single can find his or her place in the church—or the average church can figure out the best way to effectively deploy singles into ministry.

When it comes to singles in kingdom work, we're all a little disoriented.

Many single Christians have been using the wrong coordinates. Their map tells them that being unmarried amounts to being uncredentialed. They'll forever be under-qualified for essential kingdom work because they have no spouse.

Likewise, many churches and Christian organizations have also been relying on faulty coordinates. Their maps tell them that being married is essential to ministry and leadership. Therefore, singles, regardless of their maturity or dedication, belong here but not there. There are limits to where they can serve and what they can do.

Hi. I'm Lewie and I'm single. I've never been married. I'm passionate about disciple-making, and because the church needs every disciple to be a disciple-maker, I'm determined to see that singles are equipped and included in the mission of the kingdom.

Now before we go any further, I want to assure you that this issue is a burden on my heart, not a chip on my shoulder. For the most part, my personal experience as a single in ministry has been quite positive. I've felt wanted, heard, and valued in every ministry role I've occupied. But sadly, I've learned that this is an exception.

Until a few years ago, writing on this subject was not on my list of things I felt I needed to do. However, the more I interacted with other singles in seminaries, churches, and missions, the more discouragement I encountered among them. This book is my attempt to take an honest and biblical look at the situation and hopefully provoke a conversation that will move us toward healing and recalibration.

When the Church Was Young

Singles had significant roles in the early church. So when we take on this subject, we're not looking for something new. We're celebrating what God has done through the lives of tens of thousands of his servants—both married and single—to take the gospel to the ends of the earth.

In the first century, singles not only led the expansion of the good news of the kingdom of God, but they also served as role models for new followers of Jesus. Since many singles laid the foundation for the spread of the gospel for centuries to come, my prayer is that the empowerment of singles will revitalize the expansion of the kingdom of God for future generations—until the return of our Lord.

To begin, let's consider the role of one man who was instrumental in the life of the young church—a man who is a timeless example of courage and humility: Barnabas.

Barnabas was a leader in the (then) new movement we call Christianity. He was also aware of emerging leaders at times when his ministry colleagues apparently were not.

Barnabas was also, presumably, single.

Saul was also a single who had come to believe in Jesus as Messiah while walking on the road to Damascus. Later, he went to Jerusalem but could not establish a relational connection with the fellow believers in the city, nor could he gain a toehold in ministry. The disciples in Jerusalem could not bring themselves to believe that Saul could possibly have become a follower of Jesus. His reputation as a deadly persecutor raised the question whether this gospel could change the heart of someone so notoriously menacing.

> When [Saul] came to Jerusalem, he tried to join the disciples, but they were all afraid of him, not believing that he really was a disciple. But Barnabas took him and brought him to the apostles ... So Saul stayed with them and moved about freely in Jerusalem, speaking boldly in the name of the Lord. (Acts 9:26–28)

Barnabas intervened on Saul's behalf, convincing the apostles that Saul had indeed become a passionate follower of Jesus. Barnabas was so persuasive that in addition to accepting Saul as a brother, the apostles welcomed him into their ministry circle. He now had a place at their table.

While still in Jerusalem, Saul boldly proclaimed that Jesus was the Messiah which resulted in threats to his life. The persecutor became the persecuted. The apostles then helped him escape the imminent danger and flee to his hometown of Tarsus—over 350 miles to the north (Acts 9:30).

Five years passed, but Barnabas did not forget Saul. When news came of the gospel's spread into new territories, including the city of Antioch, the church in Jerusalem dispatched Barnabas to help the new believers there. He soon realized that Saul could be a key man in the work, and then made the arduous journey to Tarsus to find Saul and bring him into the ministry that was occurring in Antioch.

> Then Barnabas went to Tarsus to look for Saul, and when he found him, he brought him to Antioch. So for a whole year Barnabas and Saul met with the church and taught great numbers of people. The disciples were called Christians first at Antioch. (Acts 11:25–26)

Although Saul had been set apart by God for ministry (Acts 9:15–16) and had been divinely gifted for the work, God needed a willing person, a human agent, who was ready to engage in a holy assignment to intervene on Saul's behalf. This was the second time God called upon Barnabas to get the job done. The first time, God needed to get Saul connected to the apostles in Jerusalem. Now, God needed to relocate Saul from Tarsus to Antioch. And because God had given him the ability to recognize Saul's emergence as a kingdom builder, Barnabas once again encouraged his friend and brother to join the work.

For the next year Barnabas and Saul, both single men, taught and impacted many people in Antioch. It was at this juncture that the Holy Spirit sent them on their first mission journey. And the rest is history. Notable history.

Let's pause here to ask a few what-if questions:

- What if Barnabas had not intervened for Saul in Jerusalem?
- What if Barnabas had been unwilling to make the difficult journey to Tarsus to look for Saul and to recruit him to the Antioch ministry?
- What if Barnabas ignored the Holy Spirit and never engaged with Saul at all?
- And what if Saul had said no?
- What if the apostles had made marriage a requirement for leadership?

We could also add Timothy and Titus to the unmarried leaders of the young church. In fact, much of the activity recorded in the New Testament involved singles. If we continue to track the ministry of Paul and his team over a twenty-year period, as recorded in the book of Acts, we'd surely see that there were other singles who joined in this kingdom movement.

The role of singles in the growth of the church cannot be overstated, but it is often overlooked.

Which makes me wonder how many key team members we are failing to recruit, train, and send today.

Are There Others?

Beyond the biblical record, history is well populated with singles who answered God's call and served the kingdom. Many of these have been crucial to the expanse of the gospel and to the growth of the church, including:

- John Stott (1921–2011)—Rector of All Souls Church in London; theologian and prolific author; in 2005, *Time* magazine listed him in their "100 Most Influential People in the World"
- Richard Charles (Dick) Lucas—Rector of St. Helen's Bishopsgate (1961–1998); founder of Proclamation Trust
- Amy Carmichael (1867–1951)—missionary to India for fifty-five years without taking a furlough; founder of Dohnavur Fellowship, a home for rescued children
- Vaughan Roberts—Rector of St. Ebbe's in Oxford; Director of Proclamation Trust
- Charlotte Digges "Lottie" Moon (1840–1912)—one of the first unmarried women sent by the Foreign Mission Board of the Southern Baptist Convention; served in China for thirty-nine years
- Ed Shaw—Pastor of Emmanuel City Centre in Bristol, England; author of *Same-Sex Attraction and the Church: The Surprising Plausibility of the Celibate Life*; member of the editorial team at Living Out

So, there I stood in front of a few hundred adult singles in an auditorium in Calgary, Alberta. They had come to be encouraged and to discover together how they might follow through on their commitment to serve in the kingdom—and yes, even to lead. They were not there to find a spouse or to bemoan their singleness. They were not there to be coaxed into accepting their lot as less-thans in kingdom work. They were not there to gripe.

They were there because they dared to hope that churches, seminaries, mission agencies, and other gospel-centric organizations would soon be ready to welcome them into their ranks.

I'm pretty sure there was a Barnabas or two in the room.

2

The Bias

If you have ever served on a pastoral search committee, you know how arduous the process can be. You might review hundreds of resumes, watch hours of sermons, and log mile after mile of travel for interviews and in-person meetings. In addition to all that activity is the prayer-saturated burden you carry because of the love you have for your church and your family. You long to find just the right person who is properly trained, sufficiently experienced, and has no questionable marks from past ministry activity. After all, you're going to put your own soul under this person's care. You're expecting him to teach the Scripture with accuracy and passion, and to be able to counsel, encourage, and correct.

Few others will have as much influence on you as your pastor will. You had better choose wisely.

So, what if, after months of searching, praying, listening, and discussing, you finally find a candidate who meets every biblical qualification and checks every box on the search committee's list? Every box, that is, except one: marital status. He's single.

Would you hire him?

There are churches and organizations that see 1 Timothy 3 as evidence that a pastor or elder must be married. Here the apostle Paul writes, "Therefore an overseer (elder) must be above reproach, **the husband of one wife** …" (1 Tim 3:2). Paul could have said that an overseer must be married, but he does not. Or he could have said that an elder cannot be single, but he does not. The emphasis in on the fact that *if* an elder is married he is devoted to one woman, his wife.

Theologian William Mounce comments:

> The interpretation that the phrase "the husband of one wife" means that an overseer must be married should be rejected. The counterarguments are as follows: (a) the emphasis of the phrase is on the word μία, "one," and not on the marital state; (b) Paul and Timothy would not be eligible to be overseers; (c) it runs counter to Paul's teaching that being single is a better state for church workers (if they have the gift; 1 Cor 7:17, 25–38); (d) this line of reasoning, to be consistent, would have to argue that the overseer is required to have more than one child since τέκνα, "children" (v 4) is plural; and (e) most adult men were married so it would have been a moot point.[1]

---

[1] William D. Mounce, *Word Biblical Commentary, Volume 46: Pastoral Epistles* (Nashville: Thomas Nelson Publishers, 2000), 170–71.

Or imagine you are a member of the selection committee for a mission-sending organization. A key part of your job is to screen applicants and suggest the best of the best for strategic placement. In the process you are tasked with filling a post in a newly opened field. Preparatory evaluations have shown slight to moderate risks in the area. Your agency has decided to place a team there for two years to build relationships with the handful of believers who are known to live there and to determine what long-term plans should be made for the region. Your task is to vet fourteen applicants and recommend a core team of six.

Of the many applicants you interview, two rise to the top. One is particularly well qualified. She is seasoned, proven, and committed. She is everything you would want for a team going into a new mission. She's also single.

Would you send her?

When I began researching singleness in the context of ministry placement, especially in leadership roles, a friend warned me that this was an emotionally charged topic in American evangelicalism. As a team leader in a major mission agency, he would know. Even so, I initially brushed his cautions aside since my personal experiences had been so positive. But the more interviews I conducted with singles the clearer it became that many had deep feelings of being marginalized by the church and Christian organizations.

Their feelings were then validated through the interviews I conducted with church and parachurch leaders. Frankly, I encountered a shocking level of bias. Even many of the leaders who I knew personally had disparaging things to say about singles, including:

- "Lewie, don't you think singleness is nothing more than protracted adolescence?"
- "My experience is that overall singles are immature."
- "You have to admit that older singles are strange." (That one stung. I think the man who said it forgot he was talking to an older single.)

Sometimes it was all I could do to hold my tongue, knowing that many churches have more than their share of immature married people. And strange ones too. But I was conducting these interviews to listen and learn, so thankfully I kept those thoughts to myself ... until now.

As I became more and more aware of the bias toward singles that existed in many ministry settings, I often wondered: Would this organization even hire Paul?

Seriously, if they had been interviewing candidates to join their ministry team, especially as a leader, I wasn't at all sure that the great apostle himself would have made the cut.

Imagine Paul submitting his resume. After the first review, his application is moved to the short stack because of his experience and persuasive communication skills. But he also has a worrisome past, including an unusual conversion story, the initial reluctance of many church leaders to accept him, and public conflicts with previous ministry colleagues ... not to mention his pre-conversion history of inciting violence against the very people he now wants to join.

Of course, these facts would put any search committee on edge. But even if they believed Paul truly was a changed man, and even if they were convinced that God was already using him effectively (that's an understatement), they'd still have to deal with his marriage status: single. And an older single at that.

For many, that would be a deal killer. Maybe not in your church or organization, but in many places, it would be because of the widespread view that says marriage is God's stamp of approval. If you have it, then God has fashioned you for leadership and greater responsibility, but if you don't, your options are limited.

So, what are we really talking about here? Do I think the church is anti-single? Of course not. Do I think that marriage is the path God has for most people? Yes. If you say that marriage is a good gift from God and should be esteemed, I say I agree. After all, God uses marriage to illustrate the love covenant between Christ and the church. But even those in strong and loving marriages will tell you that being someone's spouse is not the key marker of their identity. Moreover, nowhere in the Bible is marriage established as the benchmark of Christian maturity.

Unhappily Ever After

From early childhood, romance and marriage are dangled before us as the ultimate human experience. You need only go to the movies to see the evidence.

Many of us grew up with stories of romance. Think *Sleeping Beauty*, *Cinderella*, *Beauty and the Beast*, and others like them. They captured our imaginations and promised both girls and boys that someday, when they fall in love and get married to their gallant prince or beautiful princess, they would live happily ever after. Or that marriage would be the reward for heroism.

I'm not knocking these stories, but I am suggesting that at least two problems result from the expectations they raise:

1. This type of narrative can replace God in the hearts of children with the idol of romance and marriage. If you achieve these, you're a winner. But if you don't, there will be no castle or crown in your future. (Not to mention what this child will grow up to believe about a God that would withhold such a good thing from him or her.)
2. Because these stories are layered in innocence, believers are just as influenced by them as anyone; they have largely bought into the notion that *marriage = achieving the dream*, whereas *singleness = missing out*. In effect, singles are either pitied or ostracized.

Christian *singles* who fall prey to these expectations find it nearly impossible to believe that God can use them in any significant way. *Married people* who imprint these expectations on their single friends will push them to pursue marriage over godly contentment. And *leaders* who hold these expectations as qualifications risk missing out on some of the best players they could have on their team.

Please do me the favor of reading the previous paragraph again, because I want to be clear that I don't see this as a problem for ministry leaders only. Many singles have contributed to the situation; they have benched themselves and have either minimized their kingdom service or put it on hold until they get married.

Rite of Passage

I'm convinced that much of the confusion related to singles in modern-day Christianity is the result of viewing marriage as a rite of passage. While singles can be respected business owners, civic leaders, teachers, politicians, healthcare professionals, and the like outside of the church, within the church these same singles are often viewed as adolescents. We are comfortable with singles having responsibility—and even authority—in our secular lives, but we don't think of them as being qualified for spiritual leadership in the church.

We'll talk more about a theology of singleness in chapter 4, but for now I'll put this question to you: As followers of Christ, do we or do we not believe that God's will for some of his children is that they remain single? And do we or do we not believe that in such cases their singleness can be thought of as a "gift"—a way that he has uniquely positioned them for serving and leading?

Let's look at this from a Christian parent's perspective, because I understand that the thought of the gift of singleness can bring personal challenges. While a parent might agree that singleness is God's way for some, that same parent may struggle with disappointment if God chooses singleness for their child. Let me appeal to you to maintain a kingdom-focused approach to your childrearing, including the marital status of your children.

I have heard parents tell their children that they have been praying for their spouse even before the child was born. This is a good thing, in my opinion, if the parent also prays for the child with the understanding that God may have a life of singleness in mind for them, or an extended season of singleness. Are these same parents willing to consider whether marriage is a part of God's plan for their child? While praying for that future spouse, why not also offer prayers of blessing and surrender on the child's behalf, asking God to give them the joy of knowing him and loving him regardless of whether they are married?

Completeness is made possible because of Christ and the cross, not because of wedding vows and marriage licenses. When parents assume that marriage is a rite of passage, then the family dynamic can suffer unnecessarily if their son or daughter does not get married. The parents may never be able to see that child as a complete adult, and the adult child will long for an identity that evades them because dad and mom think they have not yet reached maturity. This could even drive single sons and daughters to marry the wrong person or to get married too soon just to appease their parents.

Although we know nothing about the parents of Barnabas and Paul, it's hard to imagine they would be disappointed in their sons being single, given their role in spreading the good news of the gospel throughout the Roman Empire. And though I'm confident that Timothy's grandmother, Lois, and mother, Eunice, missed him terribly when he left to travel with the apostle Paul, because they were women of faith, they were surely pleased that Timothy became a role model for believers in those early years of Christianity.

What Bob Said

Knowing of my research on singles in ministry, my brother-in-law suggested that I meet with Dr. Robert Crooks, a 92-year-old man who had never married. Bob, as he was known to his friends, had been a professor of business management at Queens College in Brooklyn until his retirement in 1979.

Though I assumed he would have plenty of wisdom to share, I was apprehensive to put a man of that age through an interview. Even the physical strength it would require to get to our meeting would surely put a strain on him (he insisted on coming to me). My apprehensions grew as I watched him shuffle up the sidewalk behind his walker and then require assistance to get up the porch steps. But it soon became clear that though feeble in body, Bob was mighty in spirit and mind.

I quickly learned that Bob had become a follower of Christ in his twenties and had spent most of his adult life in New York City. He later returned to Wichita to live out his retirement years with his brother.

When we got to the topic at hand, I asked Bob if he had given much thought to singleness and the kingdom of God. He answered with a slight smile, "Only for about 70 years." He then spoke with the conviction of a prophet.

"I tremble to think," he said, "of the dire consequences that evangelicalism has brought upon itself and the world because of its marginalization of singles out of leadership. ... We seem to have no place today for singles like Barnabas, Paul, Silas, Titus, Luke, and Timothy to lead the expansion of the kingdom of God as they did in the first century."

Later in the conversation, Bob turned his thoughts to the singles themselves: "My problem is not with the married couples with children that lead our churches and our Christian organizations. My problem is with singles that are not living up to their kingdom role of faith, risk-taking, and leadership. If kingdom singles would lead as they should then married folks and other singles would follow them just as they followed Paul, Titus, and Timothy."

I met a kindred spirit in Bob. We are in full agreement that there's plenty of work for us all to do if we're going to get every player on the field. We need the pastors, search committee members, recruiters, and mission agency leaders to stop viewing singleness as a disqualification. And we need singles to report for duty, as it were—to view their singleness as an opportunity rather than a setback.

What Dave Said

After I spoke to a gathering of church planters in the Chicago area, Dave approached me and said, "I just didn't know. Please accept my apology for my obliviousness toward singles." I had met Dave before, so I knew the backstory to his comments and apology. In fact, this was really a continuation of a conversation we'd had some time before.

Dave and his wife had served in Uganda for over twenty years before returning to Chicago to plant a church. In our previous conversation he had told me about some of the problems they had encountered with singles on their ministry team. When I asked if he had also had any problems with married people on the team, he looked back at me with that deer-in-the-headlights look. Though I hadn't meant it to be one, it was a "gotcha" moment for Dave. He was beginning to understand that the difficulties he'd had with single people were not because they were single, but because they were … people.

Overall, I find that church leaders, like Dave, are not anti-single but are simply: (1) misinformed or uninformed about the role of singles in the Bible and church history, and (2) have therefore developed shaky assumptions about marriage and singleness. I'm pleading with the church to consider what could be gained by facing the bias that has made marital status a make-or-break issue in roles of leadership. As long as we ignore the bias, as long as we are unwilling to even consider that it might be true of *us*, our internal growth will be hindered, and our outward influence will be reduced.

3

The Invisible Single

Chapter 1 gave us an overview of the role of singles throughout church history, dating back to its earliest days. In chapter 2, we pulled back the curtain to see the uncomfortable and unhealthy reality of a bias that often exists toward singleness in many churches and Christian organizations today.

In this chapter, let's take a more detailed look at how this bias can play out in the lives of unmarried believers and how their relationship with the body of Christ can suffer as a result. As we approach this deeper look, it's important that we understand the universal desire to simply "belong." Every human wants to be connected to other humans—in more than superficial ways.

Where Do I Belong?

I live in a four-flat apartment building with twelve others; we have chosen to live together as we seek to follow Jesus in community. When the lethality of COVID-19 became real to us, my friends, who are all younger than me, protected me by: (1) not allowing me to leave the apartment, and (2) by asking others not to visit me. They did my grocery shopping, picked up my prescriptions, and ran errands on my behalf. One of the men actually moved out of the apartment for my sake because his job was considered high probability for COVID-19 exposure, and he didn't want to bring the virus home to me.

If ever I felt like I belonged, it was during those long months of restricted movement—enforced out of love by a group of brothers who simply wanted to keep me alive and healthy. (I admit that I didn't always enjoy being quarantined. Cabin fever took over one evening while I was watching a documentary on elephants. At one point a pride of lions was stalking the herd and the adult elephants formed a tight circle around a calf to protect it from harm. Instead of appreciating their bravery, all I could think of was how claustrophobic it must have been for that little one to be imprisoned by a bunch of mammoth-sized legs and trunks!)

But claustrophobia and cabin fever aside, I'm certainly thankful for the protection that came through my belonging. To belong is to be bound to others by ties of affection, interdependence, and allegiance. We are made to belong. Brene Brown writes:

> A deep sense of love and belonging is an irreducible need of all people. We are biologically, cognitively, physically, and spiritually wired to love, to be loved, and to belong. When those needs are not met, we don't function as we were meant to. We break. We fall apart. We numb. We ache. We hurt others. We get sick.

On a personal level, it has been through my exposure to cultures that were once unfamiliar to me that really opened my eyes to the importance of belonging.

The Nigerian Way

My brother-in-law is Nigerian. It has been fascinating to learn some of his culture's traditions. In fact, he and my sister observe some of those in the way they raise their children.

Two Nigerian traditions have especially interested me: (1) the naming ceremony, which is held eight days after the child's birth, and (2) the rite of passage to adulthood ceremony that is held on the child's thirteenth birthday.

I've been privileged to attend these ceremonies for my nieces and nephews. But when I realized that I wasn't fully appreciating the significance, I asked my brother-in-law to tell me more—specifically about the naming ceremony. He explained that each child is given five names, one being their dad's name, and the others being their grandparents' and great-grandparents' names). "It is all about belonging," he said. "My children will someday be attached to their children and grandchildren because they themselves are connected to their grandparents and great-grandparents."

Their names connect family history to family legacy; reaching back enables the child to reach forward.

The Jewish Way

I live in a Jewish neighborhood. Each year we are invited to join our Jewish friends in celebrating the festival of Sukkot (aka the Feast of Tabernacles). This is a joyous four-day celebration of the harvest and a time to remember Israel's wandering in the Sinai desert before entering the promised land. The observants build a temporary shelter (*sukkah*) in their backyard to represent the tents that the Israelites lived in while traveling through the wilderness.

As part of the Sukkot tradition, the parents and grandparents sit in the *sukkah* with the children and tell stories of their ancestors going back six generations. This is done so that the children will always know from where they came and to whom they belong.

Now that I've experienced these cultural observances, I realize that we lose out when such multi-generational traditions are not kept. Life-shaping connections are lost. Too much independence weakens us.

I also believe that if there is a "culture" where belonging should be the normal experience, it is the church. Do you agree? I'm certain that Jesus and the apostle Paul both thought so.

Jesus prayed to the Father: "I pray also for those who will believe in me through their [the disciples'] message, that all of them [all believers throughout all time] may be one, Father, just as you are in me, and I am in you" (John 17:20–21). Just as Jesus and the Father are one, so Jesus prayed that all who believe in him would be one; that in belonging to the same Father they would know their connection to one another.

When Paul wrote to the church in Rome about the various gifts of the Holy Spirit, he emphasized, "so in Christ we, though many, form one body, and each member belongs to all the others" (Rom 12:5). Paul wants everyone in the church to understand that their differences—which are designed by God—actually connect them. They belong to one another. Each one is needed by the rest.

Irrelevant, Invisible, and Immature

Through the teaching and prayers of Christ and the writings of Paul, we know that every person in the body of Christ is vital. Each one is relevant to the *health* of the church and the *mission* of the church. (The only exceptions are those who choose to continue living in sin after the Holy Spirit calls them to repent and they refuse. In such cases, the church can exercise biblical authority which in some drastic instances could lead to withholding fellowship from the offenders. But even these measures will hopefully be temporary, when repentance triggers restoration.)

It is therefore a horrible feeling for a Christian brother or sister to be given the impression that they are irrelevant. But sadly, this is the sense that many singles have. Many times I have heard the word *invisible* used when I ask singles to describe how they see themselves in the eyes of their church or mission agency, especially their leaders.

I'm not sure how widespread these feelings are, but I heard them voiced often enough to realize that there is a problem that needs our attention. Wherever the attitudes exist that push singles aside, they weaken the body of Christ. Such perspectives not only harm those we are called to love but also sideline them from being vitally involved in God's work.

Singles are often looked on with a form of pity that is far from compassionate. Though cloaked behind smiles and misguided encouragement, such assurances that "someday the right one will come along," exposes the corrosive idea that singles somehow lead inferior lives. I'm reminded of what a single lady in her mid-thirties told me happened one evening at her Bible study group. A woman announced her engagement and was immediately met with cheers, congratulations, and hugs from the group. And then the leader stood up and said, "Congratulations Brenda. I'm glad to see you make the mature choice to get married."

You can imagine the message this sent to the unmarried who were there, and to the married for that matter. Once again, marital status was equated with spiritual maturity—an outlook without biblical support.

In the interviews I conducted, it was rare to find an unmarried person who felt that he or she had been empowered by their church elders or the leaders of the Christian organization wherein they served. Many were accepted and loved—which is great—but few were empowered. There seemed to be a stigma attached, sending a message that they were too immature or too incomplete to be entrusted with the weightier responsibilities of leadership.

*Non*recognition

Because our identity is partly shaped by the recognition we receive from our immediate social setting, Charles Taylor warns that "nonrecognition or misrecognition can inflict harm, can be a form of oppression, imprisoning someone in a false, distorted, and reduced mode of being."[2]

---

2 Charles Taylor, *Multiculturalism: Examining the Politics of Recognition* (Princeton: Princeton University Press, 1994), 25.

Many of the singles I interviewed have known all too personally this lack of recognition from their church and the painful discrediting from fellow believers who viewed them as "less than whole" individuals. It comes as no surprise then that a great many singles have concluded that church or ministry is not the place for them.

The issue of nonrecognition goes beyond accepting or not accepting the singleness of a person. Churches are quick to accept singles into their congregations. But there is a significant difference between being accepted and being valued. To value a single, a church or organization would say, "We have a deep appreciation for your singleness and believe it plays a vital part in our mission." That same church's or organization's members would also be willing to submit to the spiritual authority of a single when appropriate.

Though I've referred several times to the interviews I've conducted, my thoughts are not merely anecdotal. Consider this indication of evangelicalism's nonrecognition of singleness: About 50.2 percent of American adults are single (that's 124.6 million people). In 1950, that number was about 22 percent.[3] For the first time in American history there are more single adults than married adults, yet this is not reflected in our church attendance. Single adults make up a small percentage of our congregations.

Churches reach out to African-Americans, Asians, and Hispanics so that their congregations may reflect their cities and neighborhoods, and yet rarely are churches intentional to attract single adults even though they make up half of the adults in their "mission field." In all of this, are we not in conflict with God's value of singles?

---

[3] https://theworld.org/stories/2014/09/12/singles-now-outnumber-married-people-america-and-thats-good-thing.

*Mis*recognition

*Non*recognition is mostly a matter of neglect; *mis*recognition, on the other hand, is a deliberate marginalization. This makes it an even more troubling issue.

The misrecognition of singles is detrimental to singles, the church, the world, and the kingdom of God. Singles who are in Christ are part of the church, so what affects these singles affects the whole church, and what affects the church affects the singles.

But rather than viewing singles from a biblical perspective, the prevailing attitude within the evangelical church is characterized by skepticism. I suspect that this attitude is not often based on actual experience but on learned presupposition; we've trained ourselves to see singles as people who are "without." Since they are "without" a spouse, they must be "without" the qualities that would make them fit for marriage. When meeting a single, the question that occurs to many is: What is wrong with them?

In fairness, it is natural to wonder why someone is single, given that many individuals choose to marry. However, I propose that it would be better, and certainly more Christlike, to not have negative assumptions about an unmarried person, but rather we should seek to know them, in an appropriate manner, of course. Could they be a modern-day Timothy or Titus? Perhaps their singleness is due to God "setting them apart" for a kingdom assignment rather than "setting them aside" due to some deficiency? And could it be that God has something he wants to teach you through them? Or do you assume that their marital status makes them less mature than you?

To be sure, there are a great many immature, emotionally unhealthy, and sexually promiscuous singles. But it would be an error to assume these traits are true of all or even most singles. The truth is that these issues are just as prevalent among married adults. Marriage doesn't bring an end to sin.

Let me close this chapter with an abbreviated list of the ways that singles in the church have experienced misrecognition. I'll challenge each of these with a corresponding truth.

Misrecognition #1: *Singles tend to be strange.*

Truth: *Peculiarity is not limited to singles.*

I admit that I have met some strange singles over the years, but I have known some peculiar married people, too. Marriage does not eradicate strangeness and in some cases seems to exacerbate it.

Singles can serve as godly role models for all believers to follow. Paul, Barnabas, Silas, Timothy, and Titus served as examples for the new believers to imitate in the first century. In more recent times David Brainerd, John Stott, Amy Carmichael, and Henrietta Mears have all inspired Christianity by their example.

Misrecognition #2: *Singles are sexually promiscuous.*

Truth: *Marriage does not ensure sexual purity.*

The presumption that marriage ensures sexual purity is held in tandem with the presumption that singleness is the cause of promiscuity. Spiritual leaders should be diligent to ensure the moral virtue of singles in their care, but no more than we would want them to ensure the purity of married couples. And as hard as it is for some people to believe, it is possible to be single and to live a joyful, chaste, sincere, and holy life.

Most should marry and enjoy God's good gift of matrimony but being married does not guarantee sexual purity. Sadly, there are husbands and wives who continue to "play the field" even though they have vowed not to.

Misrecognition #3: *Singles are incomplete individuals.*

Truth: *Singles are whole individuals when the risen Messiah lives within them.*

At one point in my research for this book, I concentrated my interviews on singles who were thirty-five years old and above and in full-time ministry. One interviewee said, "As a single I am not a 65% person or an 80% person but because of Jesus within me I am a 100% complete individual. It is Jesus who makes a person complete and content, not marriage." Another said, "I just want people to stop feeling sorry for me because I am single! It is condescending for others to think that I am disadvantaged as a single."

It is an affront to the heavenly Father to feel sorry for a single person whom the Lord has blessed with the good gift of singleness. It is also presumptuous to think others must desire the same thing we do. Should a person feel bad for desiring to get married? Certainly not, but neither should married people assume that singleness is a lower or lesser identity.

Misrecognition #4: *Singles are doomed to live with discontentment.*

Truth: *Marriage does not guarantee contentment.*

Unhappy singles are often more vocal and visible, and therefore more memorable, than those who are content. So, there is a tendency to think that discontentment is a marker of singleness. But just as there are singles whose unhappiness is public information, the same is true of the married community. And the plethora of books, podcasts, events, and other resources that are dedicated to marriage restoration indicate that spouses are struggling just as much as singles are; perhaps more.

Misrecognition #5: *Singles are fickle and irresponsible.*

Truth: *Marriage does not equate maturity. There are singles who are trustworthy and who model godly character.*

Nowhere else in American society are singles separated out as they are in the Protestant church. Although there are many aspects of our lives that we entrust to singles (pilots, nurses, doctors, bosses, or accountants could all be single), when it comes to our spiritual lives we hesitate to recognize the leadership aptitude of singles.

Just as married people will (or will not) establish their faithfulness to the Lord over time, so a single will do the same. The disciples in Timothy's hometown of Lystra recognized his spiritual uniqueness and based on their recommendation, Paul invited Timothy to minister alongside him in a ministry partnership that lasted for years (see Phil 2:22).

Misrecognition #6: *Singleness limits ministry opportunities.*

Truth: *Singleness opens opportunities not accessible to those who are married and have children.*

Singleness is not a constraint. There are ministry opportunities that married couples, especially those with children, cannot attempt. I will say more about this in chapter 5.

Misrecognition #7: *Singleness inhibits ministry effectiveness.*

Truth: *The Holy Spirit is as effective through singles as through married people.*

In the first century, singles were entrusted with the responsibility of the expansion of the kingdom of God on earth. Barnabas, Paul, Silas, Titus, Luke, and Timothy led cutting-edge initiatives of the gospel in the Roman Empire. Though single, they taught the scriptures, established spiritual leaders, and led the churches.

Misrecognition #8: *God is withholding blessing from a single.*

Truth: *Singleness can be received as a blessing just as marriage can.*

God's goodness is core to his nature. We receive his goodness in many different ways, and we can always be sure that even when he seems to withhold something from us—something we had hopes and plans for—that emanates from his goodness too.

In closing, let me share this with my unmarried brothers and sisters—

Belonging will not just drop in your lap. I don't think I'm overstating it when I say there is a danger in passively waiting for it to come to you. Perhaps you are meant to *create* the community to which you are to belong. In fact, I believe that part of the giftedness for a kingdom single is to be able to create a place for others to belong. Families with children often do not have the capacity to begin a community for others. In our ministry in Chicago, the singles are the relational glue that connects our families together. So, if you are missing out on the belonging aspect of life, take up the challenge and make it happen—for yourself and for others.

4

A Theology of Singleness

We've been thinking of the role of singles in church leadership primarily through a historical lens. Let's now look through a theological one. The leading question is this: How should singleness be viewed?

To begin, I want you to hear from my friend Seth.

Seth's Story

I am 38 years old. I didn't plan to still be single at this age, but by his kindness, God has gradually led me to see my singleness as a blessing and a gift, just as much as marriage is a blessing and a gift to others.

I grew up in a Southern Baptist family with two godly parents who loved the Lord and loved me. However, I don't recall ever receiving any counsel from my parents about how I should think through the decision to marry or remain single. The idea of lifelong singleness, whether as a personal choice or as a result of God's providence, was never discussed. Mom and Dad seemed to operate under the assumption that I would grow up, get married, and have a family, which they often communicated through comments about how they looked forward to those events in the future. Consequently, I also assumed that I would get married someday.

I continued to operate under that assumption throughout high school and college, even though I didn't date very much. I reasoned that most people seemed to get married after college, and that was several years away. So why worry about it now? It made more sense to focus on school, develop good friendships, and prepare for a vocation so I could support a family. In college, I received a lot of biblical instruction about dating and marriage through Christian student organizations, but again, nothing about singleness. I can't recall ever hearing a speaker talk about singleness as a legitimate Christian calling, but it could also be that I tuned those out because I simply assumed that I would marry.

When I began seminary in 2008, I still wasn't in a hurry to get married. Then I met Naomi.

Naomi joined the small group I was leading at our church. I was attracted to her, so I took the time to get to know her. I also asked older couples at church, who knew both of us, what they thought about my pursuing her. I received nothing but encouragement. Through some incredible conversations with Naomi, I even sensed that God was encouraging me to pursue her.

So, when I asked Naomi out, I was confident she would say yes. But after taking some time to think about it, she called me back and kindly turned me down. I was stunned at first, but convinced myself that it was supposed to be and that she would have a change of heart. I had never felt this way about a girl. This went on for about two months, during which time Naomi's work schedule changed and she had to join a different small group. I saw her less and less.

Then, my confidence came crashing down one day when I saw her, obviously dressed for a date, going into a restaurant with another guy. At first it felt like my whole world had collapsed, but I would come to see it as a kind act from a loving God. I had made Naomi, and the hope of a relationship with her, an idol; it had become my source of joy and hope. And now I was beginning to experience the pain that comes from doing that.

I went through a month of intense grieving. I remember often walking into the woods to find a secluded place and spending hours praying and praising God, with tears, for his goodness to me in the midst of my pain. Before this, I only knew in theory what it meant to love God as the greatest treasure in the world, but afterward, I knew what it meant to practice and experience treasuring Christ above everything else.

God worked deeply in my heart during this time, and he simply would not allow me to comfort myself by assuming he would lead another lady into my life. I certainly wanted to comfort myself with this thought, but the Holy Spirit repeatedly convicted me that that would be the easy way out. Furthermore, I would have probably set up another idol, in place of Naomi.

God was kind enough to keep me from repeating that error, and even though in the short run it made my grief more difficult, in the long run it resulted in a far more lasting joy in Christ. The Lord gradually taught me that marriage would never give me true, lasting joy but that Christ's love and acceptance would. As one of my friends put it, "The same thing that gives you true joy and fulfillment as a single person is what will give you true joy and fulfillment as a married person." If God had allowed me to continue placing my hope and joy in the prospect of marriage, I would have missed out on his plan for finding my contentment in him alone.

After receiving my master's degree, I moved to another seminary to enter a PhD program. My dissertation would end up focusing on the Puritan pastor Richard Baxter who, quite surprisingly, argued that pastors would best serve God and their churches if they remained unmarried. I found Baxter's viewpoint interesting, mostly because it contrasted so sharply with the prevailing outlook on marriage and singleness within the church.

I found the same outlook to be true at the seminary. As I wrestled through this in my own mind and heart, I made a few observations.

1. I was alarmed at how marriage was depicted as a goal to be reached quickly, with little emphasis on how God used the deferred hope of marriage, in some cases such as mine, as a vital means of sanctifying his people. The disappointment and doubts that Christians experience while seeking a spouse can be used to wean our affections off placing our hope in things God may not desire for us and to deepen our relationship with him.

2. Because there was so much emphasis on the sanctifying effect of marriage and hardly any emphasis on singleness as a means of sanctification, there seemed to be only one path for Christians to grow into maturity: marriage. The result of this, I believe, is that single people will feel they can only achieve a subpar level of sanctification. In fact, that was precisely what a friend of mine was told by a fellow seminary student who was married. He said that he believed no single person would ever be able to achieve the same level of sanctification and maturity that a married person would!

3. Mature biblical manhood and womanhood was exclusively conflated with getting married and having a family. Once again, this can only result in viewing marriage as the only respectable state for mature Christians.

Most people will marry, so it makes sense that Christian colleges and seminaries often address the importance of God-honoring marriages. I applaud that. But I wonder what message we are sending to those who, like Seth, have been called both to ministry and to singleness. Are our assumptions keeping us from training some of God's best servants?

Theology Observed: Listening to Paul

Our view of God influences our view of singleness, just as it does with all other aspects of humanity. For example, if we believe that God does not show favoritism based on income, heritage, or ethnicity, then we can logically conclude that being unmarried should not be viewed as a stigma either.

Even though evangelicals are dedicated to a proper interpretation of the Bible and are committed to handling the Scriptures as a guide for all things, we seem to have given little thought to searching the Scriptures in regard to singleness—even though the New Testament gives it significant attention.

Of the biblical authors, Paul, an unmarried apostle, wrote the most about singleness. He wrote from personal experience and with an understanding of the key contribution singles had made in the advancement of the kingdom of God. By the time he wrote his first letter to the Corinthians, Paul was fifty years old,[4] had been a follower of Jesus for twenty years, and had been active in itinerant ministry for eight years. He would remain single another thirteen years, until his death.

---

4 The apostle Paul was born AD 6 as a Roman citizen to Jewish parents in Tarsus (in modern eastern Turkey). https://www.christianitytoday.com/history/issues/issue-47/apostle-paul-and-his-times-christian-history-timeline.html.

What Paul didn't say is nearly as informative as what he did say. He did not address singleness as a complication or as something to avoid. Rather, he spoke with contentment and authority about the joy of living an undistracted life for his Lord as a single person.

Paul had a wide range of experiences as a single, having been single as both a young man and an older man. From his thirty-fifth year through his fortieth, Paul had the opportunity to return to his hometown of Tarsus and live as a single adult among family and friends.[5] This meant being a single son to his parents, a single brother to his sister, a single uncle to his nephew, a single businessman, a single pastor, a single missionary, and a single friend.

Paul also had experience ministering alongside singles and married couples. He understood the differences between a family's approach to ministry and his approach as a single. It is obvious from his writing that he had given thought to the advantages and disadvantages of singleness and marriage in ministry.

Paul lived with the urgency of the great task before him. He understood the viability of his singleness and invited others to join him in a grand missional adventure. Though he held marriage in high regard, he also lifted the merits of singleness so others would consider how it benefited the kingdom.

> I would like you to be free from concern. An unmarried man is concerned about the Lord's affairs—how he can please the Lord. But a married man is concerned about the affairs of this world—how he can please his wife—and his interests are divided. An unmarried woman or virgin is concerned about the Lord's affairs: Her aim is to be devoted to the Lord in both body and spirit.

---

5 https://www.blueletterbible.org/study/paul/timeline.cfm.

> But a married woman is concerned about the affairs of this world—how she can please her husband. I am saying this for your own good, not to restrict you, but that you may live in a right way in undivided devotion to the Lord. (1 Cor 7:32–35)

Clearly, Paul viewed his life of singleness with joy and contentment because he was grounded in the understanding that God loved him unconditionally. God did not love him any less than his married ministry colleagues. He didn't lack credentials. Singleness did not separate Paul from the love of God, nor did it disqualify him from being a godly leader.

Theology Applied: Bringing Beliefs to Life

Paul's lifestyle and his high level of contentment demonstrate that being unmarried is neither an indication of God's displeasure nor a limitation on his designs. As I've said, God gives different gifts and callings to individuals. We should value both the gifts he has given to us and those given to others, and we should remain focused on our kingdom purpose: to make disciples.

A Spiritual Family

More than any other biblical writer, Paul used familial terminology when speaking of the relationships believers have with God and with one another. For example, he sometimes used the word "adoption" (Greek, *huiothesia*) to describe the nature of our relationship with God through Christ, emphasizing the fact that none of us come into it by birthright or merit.

Additionally, through his use of other family related language, it is evident that Paul viewed himself as a spiritual parent. He referred to Timothy as his "beloved and faithful child in the Lord" (1 Cor 4:17), "son" (Phil 4:22), "my child in the faith" (1 Tim 1:2, 18), and "my beloved child" (2 Tim 1:2). Paul also called Titus his "true child in a common faith" (Titus 1:4), and collectively addressed the believers in Corinth as his "beloved children" (1 Cor 4:14).

The family context gave Paul a way to understand and explain how life in Christ functioned, including his own identity, his role in the kingdom of God, his relationships with other believers, his relationship with God, how he led, how he ministered to people, and how believers should treat one another. Even so, family was more than a metaphor to him. Paul believed and taught that Christians are indeed part of a spiritual family. Our connection to one another in Christ is deeper and richer than any we may experience with "blood relatives'" or the families we may marry into.

Paul created spiritual families of love, belonging, healing, security, and nurturing made up of his spiritual offspring. These were not special family units that were disconnected from the larger family of God. Far from it. Most of these men and women were in the thick of building the church and expanding the kingdom. Though an unmarried man "parented" them in the faith, they were active participants in the growing movement of Christianity throughout the world.

As my friend Barry Danylak observes:

> Did Paul have children of his own? Lots of them: Timothy, Titus, and Onesimus, to name a few, and whole churches of followers of Jesus Christ. We too, like Paul, are called to be spiritual parents. Not only in begetting children through the gospel but in raising them in the nurture and admonition of the Lord until they too are

mature disciples. ... Paul's progeny were those begotten in Christ through the limitless power of the gospel for an eternal inheritance in heaven.[6]

Maturity in our physical bodies brings with it the capability to reproduce; likewise, with our spiritual nature. Disciple-making is the activity of mature believers. Spiritual parenting requires engagement, sacrifice, pursuit, long-term commitment, surrender, forgiveness, patience, understanding, and intentionality. Singles need to include themselves in this and the church needs to empower and include them. Singleness is not a restriction.

God Is Good!

I close this chapter with a few brief paragraphs about the goodness of God and how we can sometimes miss it.

God is good! I have heard many engaged people say this because they have found the one with whom they want to spend the rest of their lives. I have heard many married people say this because they love sharing their days and nights with their soul companion. I have heard many parents say this when a baby is born or one of their children accomplishes something outstanding.

They are right. God is good. And they are right to celebrate the demonstrations of God's goodness that they have experienced. But can I just state the obvious? God is also good to the never engaged, to the never married, to the single again, to the couple struggling in their marriage, to the childless couple, to the parents whose children rebel, to the ...

---

6 Barry Danylak. *Redeeming Singleness (Foreword by John Piper): How the Storyline of Scripture Affirms the Single Life* (Crossway: Kindle Edition), 142.

It is a precarious position to view God as good when only "favorable" things happen or when we get what we want. To follow this logic means that if things do not go according to our wants and plans, then God has stopped being good.

Paul got to the heart of the matter when he wrote:

> I know what it is to be in need, and I know what it is to have plenty. I have learned the secret of being content in any and every situation, whether well fed or hungry, whether living in plenty or in want. I can do everything through him who gives me strength. (Phil 4:12–13)

God's goodness does not ebb and flow with our circumstances. His goodness is stable, eternal, tenacious, irrevocable.

So, to a single who sees marriage as the "greener grass" of life, to the married couples who view marriage as a superior blessing to singleness, and to churches and Christian organizations that hold marriage as an indication of maturity and a qualification for spiritual parenting and leadership, I simply ask … Why? Why put a restriction where God has not?

5

The Kingdom-First Life

How radical does the following sound?

> I have become all things to all people, so that by all possible means I might save some. I do all this for the sake of the gospel, that I may share in its blessings. (1 Cor 9:22–23)

I'm not sure how comfortable we'd be around a twenty-first-century version of Paul. He would probably hang out with people we'd rather avoid. He'd probably spend time learning all kinds of languages and customs that we'd consider a waste of time. He might even let himself get taken advantage of … if it meant gaining an opportunity to share the gospel.

He might just be too other-worldly to be accepted into our circles.

Now, I'm not suggesting that kingdom living means we all must be excessively odd. But it will make us different. It will move us in some counter-cultural ways. Radical. Yes, that's the word—*radical*—radically normal.

Kingdom First, Kingdom Always

Each one of us has a worldview, a core set of beliefs that frames the way we approach life. Our worldview is a composite of experiences we've had, lessons we've learned, beliefs we've embraced, and wounds we've received, among other things.

Our worldview will probably have a hierarchy; certain things will matter more to us than others. For example, if our immediate family is of top importance, we will interpret nearly everything that happens around us in terms of how it affects our family. If vocational success is our top priority, our decisions will be influenced by what we believe will either advance or hinder our career. Decisions on where we live, who our closest friends are, and even our style of wardrobe are flavored by our worldview.

What I'm suggesting—and certainly I'm not the first to do so—is that in the life of a believer, no issue should rival the kingdom of God in importance. The Scriptures address this repeatedly.

> But seek first his kingdom and his righteousness, and all these things will be given to you as well. (Matt 6:33)

> What is more, I consider everything a loss because of the surpassing worth of knowing Christ Jesus my Lord, for whose sake I have lost all things. I consider them garbage, that I may gain Christ. (Phil 3:8)

> Jesus replied, "No one who puts his hand to the plow and looks back is fit for service in the kingdom of God." (Luke 9:62)

> If anyone comes to me and does not hate father and mother, wife and children, brothers and sisters—yes, even his own life—such a person cannot be my disciple. And whoever who does not carry their cross and follow me cannot be my disciple. (Luke 14:26–27)

The King and his kingdom are our highest calling and the supreme purpose of life. To unbelievers, and even to some believers, this may sound far too radical. But a kingdom-first way of living requires a kingdom-first way of thinking.

Disciple-Making

Disciple-making is the primary activity of the kingdom-first lifestyle. Because we are talking about inclusion—about being careful not to eliminate anyone from kingdom service for reasons other than biblical ones—let's think about how disciples should work together and help one another in fulfilling our mission. What is the nature of the relationship among disciples, and how does it help or hinder our effectiveness in making "disciples of all nations" (Matt 28:19)?

The expectation, when recruiting employees, is that people will be nothing more than colleagues (it's great if they become friends, but that's not required to do the job). In contrast, the kingdom of God operates on a different principle: not merely colleagues, but siblings and friends. More than being cordial to one another, more than communicating back and forth with one another, even more than cooperating with one another, kingdom men and women *love* one another. That is the central and nonnegotiable dynamic of kingdom-first living.

Consider these words of Christ:

> My command is this: love each other as I have loved you. Greater love has no one than this: to lay down one's life for one's friends. You are my friends if you do what I command. I no longer call you servants, because a servant does not know his master's business. Instead I have called you friends, for everything that I learned from my Father

> I have made known to you. You did not choose me, but I chose you and appointed you so that you might go and bear fruit—fruit that will last—and so that whatever you ask in my name, the Father will give you. This is my command: Love each other. (John 15:12–17)

Try to hear these words through the ears of a first-generation disciple. You've grown up in a relatively small community where families live in close proximity, sometimes even within the same structure or compound. You've recently broken ranks with some in your family and many in your community because you believe that Jesus is the Messiah. You're aware of the scornful looks from relatives and neighbors; you've overheard their derogatory comments. These sting, but you're committed to the Way. Not even the strong bonds of family can come between you and Christ. You hope they come to believe in him too.

Of course, this means not just having a new teacher and leader, but a new group of friends as well. To your surprise, you're experiencing friendship like you've never experienced it before. What is this attachment you feel to them, this loyalty? Could it be … love?

Sure, there's still some rivalry, an occasional harsh word, and even a tinge of frustration now and then, but none of it hangs over you like it would have in the past. You're learning what real forgiveness is. The teachings of Jesus have penetrated your mind and your heart. In the past you memorized words and precepts out of religious obligation, but these words are different, as if they are living and breathing. They make you different. You don't just commit them to memory, you actually do them.

And now Jesus is teaching you and your friends to *love one another* "*as I have loved you*" … be ready to lay down your life for one another.

That's new! That's courageous, sacrificial, you-matter-more-to-me-than-I-matter-to-me kind of love. Never saw that before. Never even imagined it.

This "new command," as Jesus called it, was something he said to the disciples while telling them he would soon be leaving. Later, when he commissioned them to be disciple makers, they already understood that love was essential to their assignment. Above all other characteristics and methods, love would be their standard of conduct and the hallmark of their credibility ... "By this everyone will know that you are my disciples, if you love one another" (John 13:35).

The Advantage of Singleness

When we are truly thinking, serving, and relating to one another in a kingdom-first way, other qualifiers that we may have intentionally or unintentionally brought into the discussion—other than biblical guidelines—hold less importance. This is a healthy move forward.

However, I am now going to contradict myself somewhat. I've been hammering the point that we should leave marital status off the qualification-disqualification list when considering ministry service and roles. Yet I also believe that there are certain kingdom assignments where singleness is an advantage. A quick revisit to the life and writings of the apostle Paul supports this, in my opinion.

> I wish that all of you were as I am [unmarried]. But each of you has your own gift from God; one has this gift, another has that. ... I would like you to be free from concern. An unmarried man is concerned about the Lord's affairs—how he can please the Lord. But a married man is concerned about the things of this world—how he can please his wife—and his interests are divided. (1 Cor 7:7, 32–34)

SINGLE-MINDED SERVICE

Paul introduced the concept that singleness might be preferable to marriage by acknowledging that he was speaking of "a concession, not a command" (v. 6). He knew it would be a strange idea to many and rejected outright by others. In that culture, to be single was often regarded as an inferior life status, perhaps even a punishment from God. But here is a prominent man of God not only endorsing singleness but actually presenting it as a contributing factor to highly effective Christian service.

A few chapters later, Paul would write: "Nevertheless, we have not made use of this right [to have a believing wife and to receive pay for ministry work], but we endure anything rather than put an obstacle in the way of the gospel of Christ." (1 Cor 9:4) He explained that he intentionally kept away from anything he believed could hinder his ministry endeavors. I find it interesting that to the apostle's way of thinking, marriage was one of those possible hindrances.

We know that Paul led a high-risk life; he was often under the threat of severe injury or death and regularly traveled by dangerous means to dangerous places. He was functionally homeless, living in a constant state of readiness to leave one assignment and move quickly to the next. Clearly, in his thinking, marriage would have made this lifestyle more challenging.

Though Paul's ministry modus operandi is not for everyone, which he himself admitted, it should be considered, especially by those who plan to serve in hard places.

Every family encounters decisions and obstacles related to basic life issues such as housing, healthcare, education, and friendships. These all become more complex for families that move overseas (or, in some cases, to certain inner city or urban areas in the US). Added to the usual family issues are other concerns that come with many mission assignments—language barriers, limited dietary options, and preparedness to mobilize quickly, to name a few.

These types of concerns are less disruptive to singles than they are to families, and that means they are generally less disruptive to the mission overall. For example, if a missionary's child needs medical care that is unavailable where they are serving, the entire family will likely have to relocate—and perhaps be unable to return. The same can happen if educational needs are not met. And if one or both spouses hold leadership roles in the mission, it can take quite some time to backfill their positions and get the work back on track. What happens to the mission momentum in the meantime?

Singleness can be advantageous, particularly in scenarios where a new field is being investigated, a new location is being opened, or in areas where danger could require evacuation on short notice. Singles are generally more nimble and better positioned to react quickly in such situations.

Most mission strategists that I am aware of are married with children, and they usually design strategies with the assumption that their field workers will be married and have children as well. I have yet to come across a mission strategy with singles in mind—which is bewildering, considering the significant role of singles in the history of the church.

Obviously, there's great need and opportunity for married couples and families on the mission field and in church planting. I am simply pointing out that there is little consideration of singles in our expansion strategy, and I think we're missing out.

A Word to Those Who Are Single in the Kingdom

Imagine the kingdom possibilities of singleness, of being one who is set apart rather than one who's been set aside. You've not been benched because you don't have a spouse or a family. The opposite could be true: you're uniquely positioned to serve in ways and in places where there is great need … perhaps even to lead in those movements.

Don't waste emotional energy wishing for what you don't have. Instead, see your singleness as a good gift from God for his glory and purpose. Worrying about being single, being bitter about it, or using it as an excuse for ministry non-involvement is not just counterproductive, it is kingdom-second thinking—*I'll do what God wants when he gives me what I want*. You could be missing out on great blessings and opportunities.

The kingdom needs you … now.

6

Being Barnabas

The bottom dropped out when my fiancée broke our engagement. That event reshaped nearly every aspect of the future I had planned.

My hopes of being a husband and dad were over. You see, I am Lewis Fitch Clark III and all my life people would say to me, "I'm looking forward to meeting Lewis the IV someday." Not only was I a disappointment to myself, but I was also letting down my parents and so many others by not producing an heir.

My ministry life was equally hopeless. What church is going to hire a single pastor?

Running through it all was the question, What's wrong with me? I did not want to live alone, and I did not want to die alone.

I compare those days after the breakup to being in a dark cave. Thankfully, months later the Lord broke through. I could still take you to my exact location where he infused hope and courage back into my heart. Isaiah 56 captures my experience.

> And let no eunuch complain,
> "I am only a dry tree."

For this is what the LORD says:

> "To the eunuchs who keep my Sabbaths,
> who choose what pleases me
> and hold fast to my covenant—
> to them I will give within my temple and its walls
> a memorial and a name
> better than sons and daughters;
> I will give them an everlasting name
> that will endure forever. (Isaiah 56:3b–5)

In the days of Isaiah's writing, having children was of great importance. A man's name, and therefore his very existence was likely to be forgotten if he had no offspring. Many people would have considered him a cursed or unworthy man, so it was just as well that he would be forgotten.

But here the Lord promises that though someone may not have biological offspring, he will give them a name that is better than sons and daughters. The Lord promises a name that will live on for generations without end.

Through this passage, God assured me that: (1) he was aware of and engaged with my circumstances as a single, (2) my situation was not hopeless, as long as I had a loving heavenly Father in my life who is powerful enough to restore me from a desperate place, (3) my responsibility was to hold fast to the Lord and to live a life that pleases him, and (4) that I could have spiritual children, grandchildren, and great-grandchildren.

More than thirty years later, I can say that the promises of God have proven true, beyond what I could have imagined. My fears about the future were unfounded. As the apostle Paul had many spiritual sons and daughters, so I have spiritual offspring around the world.

My Own Barnabas

In my college years, before my engagement and breakup, God brought a very special man into my life. Taylor Gardner was the Dean of Students at the college where I attended, and he did something for me that no one had ever done. He pursued me. Not only did he listen to me, but he encouraged and empowered me. He saw something in me that I could not see in myself.

Taylor also made a place for me. Disciples of Jesus are made by the discipler laying down his life for his disciple, as Jesus demonstrated. Taylor made more work for himself by creating a position for me to minister alongside him after I graduated. But he was willing to look beyond my youth and inexperience. He believed in me.

I'm so very grateful that all those years ago, Taylor Gardner didn't see me as an unmarried and therefore unqualified kingdom servant. He saw me as a man whom God had called and who needed to be valued and included. He was my Barnabas.

Take Down and Build Up

In 1987, President Ronald Reagan stood near the Brandenburg Gate of the Berlin Wall. Dividing East Berlin from West Berlin, the wall stood as an ideological isthmus between free democracy and Communism. That part of the world had been divided for years, but the time had come for the city of Berlin and the nation of Germany to become one again.

President Reagan's historic speech culminated with the well-known line: "Mr. Gorbachev, tear down this wall!"

I am borrowing those words to make the plea that we tear down the walls and level the boundaries that have been put in place over marital status in the kingdom of God. I'm not comparing this situation to communist oppression. But I am saying that as long as there is a restricting divide within the church, we are all weaker for it. In order to build well, we're going to first need to remove what shouldn't be there.

I encourage an honest evaluation of how your church, organization, or ministry team will consider singleness in light of the mission of the kingdom of God. Looking at the singles around you who are ready to get to work …

> Do you see them?
>
> Do you value them?
>
> Are you willing to include them?
>
> Are you willing to recruit and hire them?
>
> Are you willing to bring them in on your strategizing and planning?

If God raises them up as leaders, are you prepared to follow them?

Considering the strategic ways in which God used singles to build the church in the past, is it too far-fetched to believe he may intend to use them similarly in the future? If this is the case, what steps can you take to reengage singles in the kingdom's work?

WILLIAM CAREY PUBLISHING
visit us at missionbooks.org

Sacred Siblings: Valuing One Another for the Great Commission
Sue Eenigenburg and Suzy Grumelot

In this book, we learn about how teams come together with varying expectations of what team life should be. The authors offer ideas and positive practices of valuing one another based on a survey from 289 missionaries, representing 12 mission agencies. Read this and have your agency make moves to be better prepared for the increasingly single next generation of field workers and take action for team effectiveness now.

Learning to Lead at the Feet of Jesus: Encounters with Grace and Truth
Todd Poulter

Despite our best intentions, many of us struggle to consistently reflect Jesus in our leadership. No matter how lofty our title, status, or renown as leaders, we can never rise higher in the kingdom than to the feet of Jesus. This book highlights the rich relational setting in which Jesus exercised leadership and developed his followers into leaders. In the context of his intentional "with-ness," Jesus generously shared his life and authority with the Twelve.

Multiplying Leaders: Recognizing and Developing Grassroots Potential
Evelyn and Richard Hibbert

The Hibberts focus on how to develop grassroots Christian leaders across cultures. These often-unrecognized leaders mostly lead small groups at the growing edges of the church. They are ordinary people who faithfully share Christ amid the demands of daily life. Another focus of the book is shaping the character of developers as they humbly walk beside leaders in the leaders' community.